AF265337

MORNING IN THE WORLD

poems by
JUSTIN JUDE CARROLL

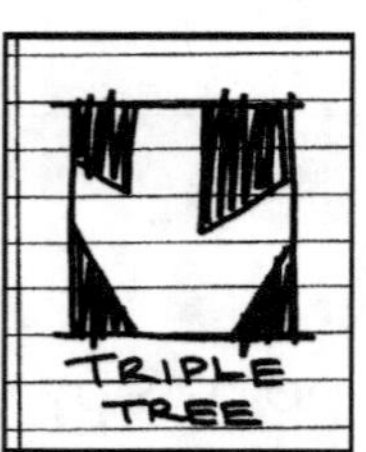

Book design by Julie Butts
Cover photo by Justin Jude Carroll
Back cover photo by Keren Rosenblum

First printed in 2018.
ISBN 978-0-692-07352-0

Contact:
justinjcarroll@gmail.com
www.justinjudecarroll.com

For Keren

I

AGAIN

The newly bare wrinkled bluffs
steam and dribble down their dust
as the last of the flood falls away.

Sun arrives, clouds glide,
mist rises from the infant cliffs. Silence.
The birds have fled high to dry their hearts.

No hoof print, vole hole, root or stem or curling thing.
No broken bone of barn nor cornerstone
of church, all borne away as if dreamed by water.

Later, slowly: Thistle. Clover, fern, young fir.
Then trillium, penstemon, bleeding heart,
green in great bouquets gathering itself.

Later still the people: Wandering in, wondering
at the steaming Eden, leaning dazed on damp stones,
prying berries from stems and after a long tidal time

felling pines for the first fence posts.

AT THE ORCHARD HOUSE

The children smuggled their treasure
in the hems of their shirts from
the tangled trees to the tub:

Thunk, thunk, each child off again
at a run, their shoes leaving
dark curls on the stone,

dandelion stars in their wake.
The sun fluttered in the west and a slack sail
of cloud came across the sky.

I was keen to join them in the limbs
but I have my place
in the kitchen drying brittle white plates,

placing them in a stack, draping the damp towel
on the wooden rack. Remembering to glance out
where the little bodies hurry. A father's way is to

drift just offshore, shine a hint of light in the mist,
however much he yearns to lean in and dash himself
on those precious wet rocks.

HALLWAYS

My five-year-old ran off the soccer field
to say he had to go potty. I was sitting at last
and wanted to sit and go on sitting.

Do you want to go by yourself? I asked. Just to see.
Yes! and before I could say *but wait*
are you sure he hurled himself away
between net and bleacher.

They say when one door closes another opens but
                         it sucks being in the hallway.
The thing is that sometimes
                    you don't know you are in a hallway

or that there are doors cupping each end
and you're a fly in a poster tube tipped
this way and that by the hands of a child.

Sometimes you wait on cold metal benches, listening
to Latin music from a distant radio, watching the boy wander

back to the field, hair flecked with water,
shins like young limbs of wood

suddenly something stronger, stranger, less yours,

here. Just now.

ON THE NESTUCCA RIVER REMEMBERING VERONA

In the morning after seeing the play in the old stone amphitheater,
    after the cool shreds of night along the parapets

of bridge, black water flaring, tallow with the light of
    a single swollen moon above red roofs—

in that stark warm morning we walked through streets
    the color of the hair on the back of the neck of

the son we had yet to dream, how his muscles
    curl and turn the head to see the heron rise

from reeds over the wandering river. So soft and ready,
    black wings gathering up air,

drifting like the ripples, finding the way into a next breath—
    We moved along the morning and into the hidden church

crouched off a crooked street, clouded with dust
    as if all its candles had cracked with age and been blown

to powder by a mystic gust from the leaded window
    and set to dancing—There we stood and thought and held

hands, parted hands, smiled at one another,
    after a time easing out into the sun, the luminous future.

THE SPLIT-RAIL FENCE

The porch and yard backed up
on a slow river moving east, tangled in swamp grass

and birch branch. On our side stood a short length
of split-rail fence bright red. I remember long before:

the slap of paintbrush on pale stripped wood.
My father didn't ask for help but I would have

traded back my two dollar allowance for
the chance to slop brush against bleeding post

over and over again. The water dreaming
past beside us. I'd have given more for

the memory of him in a damp pale-blue tee shirt
leaning on one leg, hand on hip, watching me work with

soft no-smile, not saying a word.

SIXTEEN

She'd stop and talk and talk   then laugh at her words   it was the Irish
        in her she said
we'd kiss again   her neck wet   the strings inside
it heaving a hidden weight

Most of the time I was a lonely country
to live in   that night I learned that to be filled was to
be hungrier still

Were I to make art of it
I would use strips of black felt   scattered salt
and a slip of linen falling gray down her back

WRONG WAY

Early on a Sunday, the rest of us
        coming, him going.
"This way," one would say, hooking a
        thumb, "rehearsal at nine."

The way he stood up straight,
        spread his fingers, half a
smile stumbling out. There'd been a girl, a paper
        due, he'd slept late, you know, you know.

We loved him for it: The slender shrug, "I'll be there in
        ten," how ten became thirty or more when
he slipped in between the baritones,
        mouth open to let the bright out.

All of us busy performing and there he
        was, no watch, walking his way, living.

WHEN THIS IS GONE

The world in its mirror shimmers and pulls, taut
with pause. The eagle dives from the pines to circle
the twilight. She wavers and hovers and comes around.

Water laps the hollows of my ankles, my son sprawls
in the sand watching another boy fill and empty colored drums.
The baby leans toward my fingers.

When this is gone, mosquito bites white, sunburns brown,
the water will swell on toward its one endless edge
encircling the other side of things we will not be here to see.

II

SPELL

Whatever you call it, it's here for you
now. It's caught you up or you have blundered
through as into a summer web. Fortune,
good works have nothing to do with wonder,
speech-stealing frozenness streaming like mist
not over your body but your still self,
you cannot shift teeth or curl up a fist.
Your whole You is new. No account could tell
you how to breathe or which feeling to draw
like a bead of water across cool metal,
its wet aura trailing what's left of law.
Now the clouds move on, shadows resettle.
This wish for you now and forever more:
Through every door, the whisper, the roar.

FOURTH OF JULY, PORTLAND, 2017

The arbor, the lilies all running in place,
the moths bits of tissue adrift on the wind,
the roses, lavender, whites I can't name,

a mosaic in gravel laid at the bend
and shreds of bright foil aflutter among
azalea stems and the whispering dust

blown from mimosa wings, fallen like song
to hum the cool empty streets in the dusk.
The baby's eyes full, bewildered at sky,

reposing in stroller, feet tracing stars
while brother ahead, trim shoulders held high,
cradles the soccer ball, thumb tracing bark.

The drums are all quiet. Our fires cold banked.
Tomorrow we fight, forget, or we thank.

MIDSUMMER

The grass is dry, hydrangea gray,
the treehouse black with stubborn sap,
the suet picked apart by crows.

In drawers of linen sleep the snows,
rain dreamed and gone like midday's nap.
Death hides and we forget: He stays,

draws pale lines down dark petal's face,
our sun-flecked fingers soon to chap.
He's gone, we think. We think we know.

ONE MORE MARK

Coffee cool, lake still, eagle hid
in folds of fern-gray fir across
the lake while children gauge the strings
of voice to set air humming high
and long. Splashing, gasps, cackles, *No!'s*
firework the trembling sky while
we as parents close eyes against
the obstinate dumb arc of sun,
calligraphing one more mark upon
the child's sunburned wrist, one day less
in which to scold, cajole, turn tight
tuning pegs we dared to dream our own.
Young voices sing their foreign noise;
light fades on our imagined choice.

REPOSE

True contentment makes the poem
obsolete, metaphor and form

both suborned to silver chord
that sets to trembling hidden cords

on which the world is hung and hums:
The breath, the Lord, the song, the Aum.

THE CHILD'S DREAM

I am the Light that dances.
Like all things I come and go.

The wave kisses
the sand, crumbles, dies,
a new wave rushes to kneel—
all the same ocean.

All sounds the same
sound: my breathing,
palm of my mother lightly
across my chest.

The world is the dream of
a contented child,
safe, encircled, made to know himself
holy and whole,
whose mother's love permeates him
like the swollen fullness of ocean air,
always everywhere.

She doesn't doubt and neither does
the child, and why should you?

Sleep on if it is a dream,
swell against the rocks,
someday you may wake to find yourself deep
amid the blankets under that watchful,
glowing eye.

MAKING ALWAYS MAKING

I make my way by
what is at hand.

Do not say it is half a life.
Do not say the mind of matter is the most
precious joy if you have yet to know the dumbness
of peace. Let us first live through
a moment's quiet. The crook in the neck,
kink in the spine, they are not there to be dispelled
but dissolved: Fat in a pan.
I am holed up and waiting
inside these hums and hacks, smoldering,

making, always making,
waiting for you to see.

WAIT FOR IT

God laughs.
You know it's true.

You've seen it in the dogwood boughs along the greening street.
You see it in the mirror when the morning is slow
and all lightness. The baby cries and your ears sing.

You didn't know there were such things.

That you could let out a breath while resting
on a stone patio holding a cup of sweet coffee, waiting for
the finch to find the feeder.
She comes in her time.

We all do.

Jokes make us laugh
because we are taken
by surprise.

MORNING IN THE WORLD

Harmonious hum
you hide behind
my eyes.

Light of far stars
you spill shadow
across the page.

Even talking of it does not free me of it.

There is the I who thinks about these things
and there is the world
that moves through itself,
this then that, wave and water,
inseparable: How many times
have I tried to understand it?

The trilling music in the cafe,
the baritone banter at a nearby table,
hiss of espresso,
thrum of kitchen fan,
now is the time.

Here is the way, here
is the moment
to choose not to say
what can be said.

COME, PEACE

Peace, friend.

Peace in your quest today to buy a new
pair of shoes. You are allowed
to give away the old ones
though they tear at the heel and
the wet seeps in.

Peace in your purchase
of a buttery scone, brushing
sugar crust onto the street,
taking the bite, finding
you did not want it.

Peace as you age
each second worrying, worrying:
The light is fading, the cold is coming.

Peace as my Father stands
oak-tall above you,
my Mother enfolds you
in blankets of wind,
peace in the smell of diesel and the rush of machines.
        I want to know you.
I want to know all of us.
In knowing that I may know the All.

I want the leaves, yes, but also the cloud of their colors,
the crescendo of red to gold to lavender,
the tremble of the topmost branches,

the flutter that breathes through itself. I want all of that.
I want You. In wanting You I am made without want,
I am a leaf on the path waiting for that One
to see it, pluck it up,
place it in the brown paper bag from the café,
walk on in quiet.

Peace, I know You. Peace, I am You. Peace,
I will not be mistaken for You alone, for I am
all that weaves and binds you together,
the warp of you is the marrow of me.

Come and sing with me, birds silent in the afternoon.
No truck or tire shares your song but
sing anyway, we are here, the song is us, come,
let the night come when it comes, for the day
will rise and your song will bring it forth.

Come.

ACKNOWLEDGEMENTS

My deepest thanks to Alisa Carroll for shepherding this book from the germ of an idea to a completed work. Without her dedicated support as reader, editor and project manager, this book would not have been born.

Thanks to Andrew Callard for serving as an early reader and honest friend.

Thanks to David Biespiel for early encouragement and for his slim grenade of a book *Every Writer Has a Thousand Faces*, which exploded the world of creative possibility for me.

And thanks to the Multnomah County Library for existing. Your quiet rooms made it happen.